Contents

Conker-hunting

I've always loved conkers. When I was a boy, I'd go conker-hunting with my dad.

Conkers are the seeds of the Horse chestnut tree.

conkers

Horse chestnut leaf

A seed is a tough-cased package that contains a new plant and all the food it needs to start growing.

The Seed
I Planted

Mick Manning
and Brita Granström

W
FRANKLIN WATTS
LONDON·SYDNEY

For Charles Desmond Manning

First published in 2002
by Franklin Watts,
96 Leonard Street,
London EC2A 4XD

Franklin Watts Australia
45-51 Huntley Street
Alexandria
NSW 2015

The illustrations in this book
have been drawn by both Brita and Mick

Text and illustrations © 2002 Mick Manning
and Brita Granström
Series editor: Rachel Cooke
Art director: Jonathan Hair

Printed in Hong Kong, China
A CIP catalogue record is available from
the British Library.
Dewey Classification 582
ISBN 0 7496 4301 3 (hbk)
ISBN 0 7496 4789 2 (pbk)

We'd kick up dead
leaves, give low
branches a shake.
We'd even ask
a passing squirrel.

Seeds come in lots of shapes
and sizes – from tiny grains
to big nuts. Some seeds
come in soft fruits.
Conkers come
in spiky jackets!

9

Fallen conkers find good hiding places!

To grow properly, seeds need to travel away from their parent plant.

10

They roll and bounce.
They can even float.

Some fruits are eaten by birds.
The seeds inside are
'plopped out' later!

Some seeds fall into
water and float away
downstream.

All good conker hunters know that the sticks you throw get stuck - until the wind works them loose!

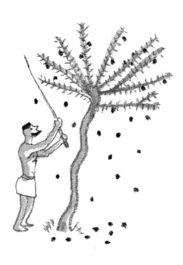

People have always used sticks to collect seeds, fruit and nuts. You have to be careful not to hit yourself, though!

Autumn winds

One autumn there
was a terrific gale.
I fell asleep listening
to the wind, and the
trees creaking . . .

Many plants – from huge
trees to dandelions – rely
on autumn winds to shake
their seeds free.

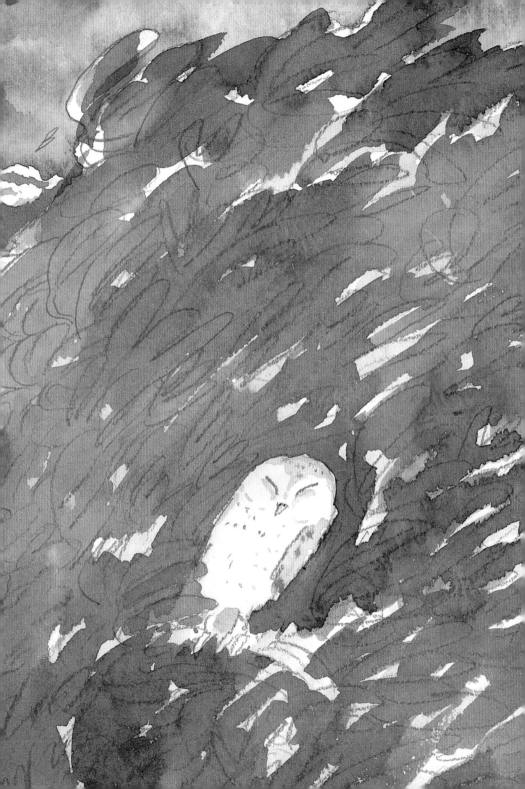

16

Next morning Dad woke me early. Pocketfuls and pocketfuls of spiky conkers lay among the fallen leaves.

We don't hunt conkers for food – but there are lots of seeds and fruits we can gather in the autumn to eat, such as hazelnuts and blackberries. Birds, squirrels and mice like to eat them, too.

Planting time

I planted my best conker.
I watered and
waited. And
watered and
waited . . .

Before it can start to grow, a conker needs some time in warm, damp, dark soil.

19

Growing

And one day it began to grow.

First came a root, then a green shoot.

Later, two tiny conker leaves unfurled.

Roots take in water and 'goodness' from the soil.

The shoot
pushes up out
of the soil.

The first leaves to
grow are called the
seed leaves.

21

A young tree is called a sapling.

Spring came. Dad scattered some seeds, and I planted out my sapling in a sheltered spot.

Spring is the best time to sow seeds and plant out saplings. The spring sunshine helps them grow.

Once a plant has its green leaves, it can make its own food with them by using energy from sunlight.

From sapling to tree

Over the years,
I watched it
grow . . .
    and grow . . .
        and grow . . .

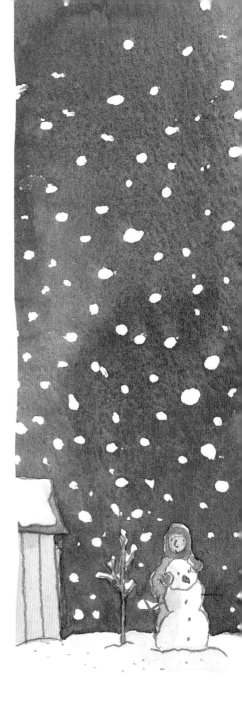

Some plants grow from a
seed, flower and die in
just a year. Some trees
take a hundred years
or more to grow.

Winter,
2 years later

24

Spring,
8 years later

Summer,
20 years later

25

Thirty years later

And I grew too!
Look! The seed
I planted has
become an
enormous tree.

Come on!
Let's go conker-
hunting . . .

Seed ideas

Find out some more about seeds - and play with conkers!

Plant a bean

Unlike conkers, beans grow quickly.

1. Line a jam jar with blotting paper and fill the jar inside it with damp cotton wool.
2. Push some broad beans between the glass and blotting paper.
3. Keep the jar in a dark place and check it each day. Don't let the cotton wool dry out.

Conker fun

Make some conker animals - or just play conkers!

string

matchsticks

Look at some seeds

Discover more about how seeds move around. Here are some examples:

Some stick to
   fur - until they
      are scratched off!

Some shoot out when
their seed pod
explodes.

Some plants shake
out their seeds like
   pepper from a
      pepper pot.

Some seeds spin from
   their parent trees on
      wings like helicopters.

Some seeds
are eaten
by wildlife . . .

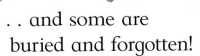

. . . and some are
   buried and forgotten!

Seed words and index